You'l. umbrel. this

VICTORIA RICHARDS

V.

Published in the United Kingdom in 2022
by V. Press,
10 Vernon Grove,
Droitwich,
Worcestershire,
WR9 9LQ.

ISBN: 978-1-8380488-8-4

Cover image and design © Sarah Leavesley, 2022.

Printed in the U.K. by Imprint Digital, Seychelles Farm, Upton Pyne, Exeter EX5 5HY, on recycled paper stock.

Acknowledgements

Sincere thanks to: Primers Volume Four by Poetry School/Nine Arches Press; Burning House Press; Hysteria 6; Cease, Cows; Ellipsis Zine; Shooter Literary Magazine; Under the Radar; Short Édition; flash & cinder; Eighty Four: Poems on Male Suicide, Vulnerability, Grief and Hope (Verve Poetry Press); #MeToo: Rallying Against Sexual Assault and harassment – a Women's Poetry Anthology (Fair Acre Press); The Hedgehog Poetry Press; Magma Poetry; Seek Poetry Magazine; WHAT MORE? PRODUCTIONS; 100 voices for 100 Years; Reflex Fiction, Pandemic Poetry Anthology; Queer Life, Queer Love (Muswell Press) and The Bridport Prize anthology 2017, in whose pages and websites some of these poems first appeared.

The opening line of "Will you please?' (p. 58) uses the opening line of Kim Addonizio's poem 'Party' from her collection Wild Nights: New and selected poems (Bloodaxe Books Ltd, 2015).

Heartfelt love and gratitude to my family – real and chosen – and to the trees in Wanstead Park.

Contents

Part I: Scattered showers

Part II: Heavy rain

Part III: Thunderstorms

Part I: Scattered showers

What are little girls made of?

a headless Barbie doll, a plastic ironing board, a nurse not a doctor, a best friend forever, a wet kiss from an uncle, a "girls can't play football", an "aren't you pretty?", an irreversible hatred of P.E, a "don't be bossy", a hand up a skirt

a bra stuffed with shoulder pads, a tear-splattered diary, a first blood at a hockey match, a Sun-In stripe, a penis on the golf course, a boy shouting "frigid", a stolen lipstick, a make-yourself-sick-if-you-want-to-be-skinny, a hand up a skirt

a pair of period pants, a pineapple Bacardi Breezer, a fast walk past a building site, the word "ugly" written in steam, a virginity out of the way, a regrettable tattoo, a size-12-on-the-bottom-14-on-top, a fag out of a window, a hand up a skirt

a shitty job, a Brazilian hot wax that hurts, a naked photo passed on without permission, a "was it even rape though?", a hangover that doesn't fade, an unwanted abortion, a "but she seemed so happy", a Facebook memorial, a hand up a skirt

an engagement ring, a Pampers advert, the smell of milk sick, a man on a train flicking his tongue, a nursery rhyme where the mummies on the bus go chatter chatter chatter, a double mastectomy, a "why's he home so late?", a hand up a skirt

a divorce, a 60-year grudge that's too late to fix, the sharp scratch of Botox, "I wish I had", a forgotten name, a reluctant diagnosis, "I wish I hadn't", a love letter that changes everything, a socially distanced funeral, a hand up a skirt

To be fifteen

and after the third can of Super Strongbow cider
to throw up in the bathroom belonging to that girl
in the year above, the one with the bra straps and dirty jokes.
She breathes in smoke without coughing, says, "alright?"
to the most beautiful boy at school, the most beautiful boy
with hair black as cats' tails, slippery as nicotine,
his smile a lopsided carousel.

To have only just started your period and to have your not-
breasts christened "pancake" by the boys who stand like
gatekeepers in the kitchen belonging to that girl. Rows
on rows of teeth. To have written a letter to the beautiful boy
and to have asked him, unthinkably, to read it.
To hear him say, "I like you – a *bit*"
like that, *bit* in italics.

To leave traces of last night's dinner
all over the pale pink shower suite belonging to that girl,
the one her parents picked from *Because You're Unique*
even though it starts with a subordinating conjunction.
To listen to her reframe this
until her words become a hurricane.
Her smile will tell its own story and she will call it truth.

Of sagging into the beautiful boy like he's the wind
and you a used tissue wearing someone else's mascara.
Of laughing chaotically at something he said
that was only half-funny, of touching his knee
and letting him touch yours, because knees are prayers
and fingers communion wafers. Of going with him
to the garden belonging to that girl. Of being ordained.

Of someone calling your parents and for your dad to come.
For him to climb the stairs belonging to that girl in silence,
force the lock while you lie foal-limbed –
to carry you out to the car like a trampled chrysanthemum.
Take you home, pull off your tights.

Wipe shame, hot and sticky, from your hair,
put a bin next to the bed for morning.

To be fifteen and have to call the house belonging to that girl.
To say sorry through sheet glass over a tongue of sand,
to rip yourself raw. To go back to school on Monday,
toes curled and desperate inside ruby slippers two sizes
too small. Childhood taps you on the shoulder –
"you're a woman, now!" To pray for an outbreak
of collective amnesia. Of mass, unexplained cardiac arrest.

To the teenage girl sobbing at the bus stop

I don't give you my coat
though your shirt is translucent with rain.

I glance sideways at the ballpoint tattoos
on the backs of your hands,

don't ask why you've scribbled out "love"
and written "sucks" instead. I'm sorry

if your friends left you to cry alone, or someone
tore your heart, made it ragged at the edges, if the person

who broke you didn't see the symmetry of your face –
your blunt black fringe, teeth white and strong as horses.

I'm sorry if your mum couldn't take care of you, or was never
taught how, or if your dad loved whisky more.

I turn my back to get away from the sky's slow dripping –
Canary Wharf a lighthouse in the distance.

Rue d'Antibes

The silhouettes the Chinese artist created
were so lifelike they drew crowds.

He seemed to take something from everyone
who posed for him, fingers slicing, whirring.

"Go on," my dad said, pushing me in front of his scissors.
He looked at me roughly and began to cut –

my outline stamped forever in black card.
Each year I came away a little less.

By fifteen, I'd lost both ears and the childish curve
of my chin. By sixteen, my lips. By seventeen, joy.

By eighteen, all that was left was scraps of black,
offcuts on the studio floor.

Prayer book

When I was twelve I found a prayer book at a jumble sale
and bought it for the grand sum of 25p. It had daffodils
on the front – a cheery bunch of yellow flowers

and I thought, "yellow flowers can only be good,
they always make people happy."
And I didn't feel happy, not very often, not even at the age

of bike rides and cupcakes and sleepovers,
of whispered secrets and first crushes and midnight feasts.
So I tried it: kneeled that night, beside my bed,

and every night for a week,
while my brother laughed and pointed,
my mother said with her voice like crushed velvet,

"she's experimenting, leave her be."
And I felt shame, and a wrongness.
And when, years later, I kneeled by a different bed

asking for forgiveness for living a God-less life,
they said – the people who'd found peace – to "turn it over",
to "surrender", but all I could think was "to who?"

Because the truth is – I didn't find God
in that jumble-sale prayer book, or in churches,
or synagogues, or Shinto shrines,

or in the mouths of lovers, or sitting by the lake,
watching swans drift past with the sun on my skin.
I didn't find God, just flowers.

Moonchildren

"Cancerians," we boasted. Best friends, born three days apart.
Water signs *with a special affinity to the moon.* At weekends
we'd sit for hours in the Pagan section of the local library,

reading books we weren't allowed to take out.
About the goddess Diana and *Old Moore's Almanac*, in print
for 200 years for those who wished they too had answers.

What were we looking for? A sense that everything
would be okay, that the fear we felt at fourteen
would grow weak, ice-crusted: would splinter

under the weight of hydrogen and helium, get smashed
to bits by the trash and debris of old space missions
floating around. The terrible fear that we wouldn't love

– be loved – that we'd never quite be seen;
that our bodies would be pinched and probed and invaded,
flags stuck inside us in a race to claim our soft spaces.

We linked arms on the way home from school,
learned to look at the floor at bus stops –
blocked out shouts of "bitch", "slut" and "oi, come here"

with glass helmets three inches thick.
Stared straight ahead at the beautiful horizon
as we orbited the local shopping mall.

Oh, how far, how distant the stars seemed
when we wanted to grow up so badly,
but gravity kept us rooted to the spot.

Two little dickie birds

Two little dickie birds, sitting on a wall. Up ahead
a pack of wolves: brazen, braying, begin their lupine call.

The birds grow quiet. Close their beaks, lower their tail
feathers, weave ribbons of cold metal through the softness
of their wings. They pre-dial 999

and the green glow of their panicked screens are fireflies,
luminescent – giving outline to the graves in the restless
churchyard. The dead watch on, mournful and alone

like the birds, their fragile hearts beating like snares
on this empty street. It is one in the morning.
The time of day when they should be falling in love,

not out of the sky like fireworks; bleeding and beautiful,
broken and dimmed, scattering ash like rain.
And the wolves keep howling,

long after it is over. After it is done. And the birds
stumble with new rings around their ankles
and the wolves laugh and send them soaring,

following the stale red scent of shame, "I told you"
and "you should have known better" back home.
Two little dickie birds, pulled behind that wall.

Fly away. Fly away. Fly away.

The one that couldn't get away

I see him in Instagram squares, hair lank against his collar,
pinned together with fine gold intent. That careful stubble,
eyes closed with Clarendon-filtered nonchalance,

gawky frame drowning in denim and on his neck
a tattoo of a cat, or lion (or a cat pretending to be a lion).
I never cared enough to commit his face to memory,

never thought about his lips. Saw his self-indulgent poetry
as self-indulgent poetry. But I remember the way
his hands felt, slippery as scales as I pretended to drink,

fresh life spawning secretly inside me. I ducked and dived
like a trout to get away from his fish-hook smile, those shark
teeth nibbling at my skin, but couldn't swim fast enough.

We too

We are Eve, we are forked tongue, we are the silky,
sex-scent of petrol, slippery on your fingers,
the fizzing *hiss crack* as you strike a match.

We are nails scratching "harder, fuck me harder"
on black velvet. We are "QUEEN", shouted from scaffold-
smashed rubble. We are that burning fire emoji,

ammonia's acrid stink. In our ring we wear split-lip rust
and our hands bleed iron. We are extra heavy flow;
we pour out of ourselves and we wash away.

You put your hands up our dresses as we walk through
Leicester Square, grab our breasts in the back of taxis,
stand too close to us on the Tube.

You whistle as we push buggies to nursery,
as we run, hot sweat metal in the park.
We are tetanus kisses

– shout "fire", nobody comes if you shout "rape" –
and we are our mothers' cries.
We are candles and oval faces, a ghost bike,

tied to a lamp-post. "What a shame.
Wasn't she pretty?" We explode with our blue flame,
and we are coming for you. We too.

Hollow Ponds

The lonely men stand by the lake, watch moorhens bob
and weave, poke plastic, a pair of swans pissed off

with the way they're always used as a symbol of perfect love,
when they can't fucking *stand* each other. Because monogamy

is difficult for anyone, let alone those who swim in circles
round and round the same wet pond.

The lonely men know this. They roll and swell
with their plastic bags. What are they waiting for?

To fuck, to be fucked, to suck, to be sucked.
To lose themselves in that frantic rutting, to drown out

their loneliness, which is never drowned out for long.
They're back again one day, three days, five hundred days

later, wearing the same nervous disappointment, boots shifting
over leaves, rollercoaster eyes, while a cardboard boat

sails past a post warning swimmers not to even *think* about
trying to wash their sins away in this hollow lake.

One of the lonely men steps forward. Scraps of toilet paper
kiss the trees, a string of condoms hangs like fairy lights.

It is his first time. Should he bite deep into rough soil,
push it throat-wards, a dirt clod embalming?

It tastes the way his teeth taste the morning after a bottle
of wine – two bottles. Some ill-advised whisky.

A goose sidles by. Unmistakeable: the slow waddling,
the casual whistle of tail feathers, tucked beneath.

The soft down hiding its secrets.

The lonely men with plastic bags hide their secrets

beneath their webbed feet. Wait for the glass-smooth
surface of the water to break. To ripple.

And a float shaped like the Starship Enterprise

Vancouver Pride, 2017

I watch them: incandescent in love, in glitter, neon tutus
around their waists like froth circling the rim of a coffee cup.

Vast expanse of desert skin, slick shimmering gold,
hair like scrub grass blurring the edges of a black ink heart.

I want to ask how it feels to love so openly, and if it hurts –
but a woman brushes past and steals the words straight

from my tongue. She wears a coat of painful nonchalance
though she's naked from the waist up, rough black tape

across her nipples, the swollen flesh beneath made sticky
with hiding. Her body flows away like water trying to escape

while a man stands on tiptoe to kiss another man; taller, stronger,
more handsome than he is, and he knows it, that first man –

wears the exquisite anticipation of being left behind
like lipstick. A stranger calls them "cute" and takes their picture

to stick in an album 5,000 miles away, to show he was here
on this day of noise and plastic water-bottle penises

and rainbow sunglasses and PRETTY BOY
stamped across narrow chests and a girl in a pink t-shirt

with a unicorn on the front that neighs and whinnies
and snorts, "I'm not gay – I'm *super* gay."

And I wonder if, years from now, the man who took that picture
will pull out the memory and turn to whoever is close

enough or cares enough to listen and say, "I was there."
And point at a small man reaching up to kiss a tall man.

Part II: Heavy rain

The whistle is missing from my life jacket

When he is born he is piscine slippery, grey and unearthly.
Black-button eyes frozen by shock-sudden roaring,
like suckerfish caught in a dull, red slipstream.

He ducks and slaps, blows bubbles,
panic-pulls the blue cord that binds and breaks us and
"I can't believe he's here.
Is he okay? Is he breathing?"

I rest my head against the rim and wait for someone to shout
       – "man overboard" –

You'll need an umbrella for this

I hold on to the handlebars of the buggy
like they're an anchor, tethering me to the pavement.

Without them I am rudderless, adrift –
my stomach full of metal wool, cutting me slowly.

No one can see me bleeding right here
on the street. They just say, "How's the baby?"

as my spleen ruptures, my liver withers, twists itself
inside out. My gums shrivel up around my teeth,

which start dropping like rain. They form pearlescent
puddles for you to crunch through. The wave

surges up, up, up and breaks over the berth of my inner ear;
my eyes leak floodwaters, red with the bodies

of billions of crustaceans who meet a slow, wet end.
How ironic – to be a creature born of sea, dead by drowning.

Your gull cry pierces the night

We struggle in each other's arms as you twist and writhe,
reel backwards, lead me in a dance across the ocean floor.
We bump against the box marked *Your First Year,*

with the blue stripes, a yellow blanket, knitted by an aunt –
the shipwreck of your cot. I let the current drag me under,
bubble-wrap tentacles wave mournfully from the ceiling.

You are angry with me. You point at the door, "da da da";
my milk chokes in your throat. What more do I have to give?
They ripped my heart from my chest when you were born,

grafted it to your back with paste and a palette knife
while they stitched me back together. It bleeds openly –
so you sleep on your front, though you're not supposed to.

In the mornings your sheets are sodden red,
my blonde, bloodied, darling boy.
You are hungry. My tears won't fill you up –

they only fall in small, dark spaces when I read something sad
on my phone about young black kids being killed in America.
Take my mind, though you might not enjoy it much;

I left it behind at an 18-course tasting menu at The Dorchester.
There was foam and something called a velouté we paid £180
for, so pretended to love, called it "rich and complex",

narrowed our eyes and nodded. It left a strange, sour taste
in my mouth, emptied me inside out. My body is hollow
but all I've got, and I don't know what else to feed you.

Tiny banshee in pale blue

You rasp and warble, weak fire in my arms.
Your cut-glass mouth.

Lonely Planet gave this 4.6 stars out of 5

When you are sick, your hot breath smokes my cheek
like a furnace. Cygnet squawk rising and falling
through the house in an unnatural swelling.
Crimson waves break over the edge of the bathtub,
tiny paper birds drown in the puddles.

I smooth your cotton hair, wear you in a ring sling –
one named *festive skies*. My spine crumbles and collapses
like the Roman ruins we saw in Bulgaria, teeming with cats.
My hips move side to side in an endless mother sway.
"Mama," you croak. "Mama."

Unthinkably, I leave you

It is cold when my alarm goes off and I dress in the half-light,
fingers fumbling laces, guts knotted like rope.
I haven't slept, not really.

Checked the time every hour, half-hoping and half-dreading
I'd hear that cough. I keep the door to your room open,
space between us stretching like a rubber band.

It is dark where you are. But in the pale blue of the baby
monitor I see the elephant lampshade, that wooden owl,
hanging from the ceiling. Then I leave you

for the taxi waiting outside, the driver calling home
to Pakistan. I leave you for deadlines and for breaking news,
to write about the weather and about other people's children

fighting for life on the opposite side of the world.
I leave you for rota, for responsibility. To sit at my desk
for an hour until my phone rings, my mother's panicky voice.

Then – running through the slow, revolving doors,
out of New Broadcasting House, down Portland Place, away
from All Souls Church. Past the black and navy suits

marching from the underground, vaulting the jagged
escalator steps in threes to take the next train east.
The road home glitters with black ice, the crack and crunch

of snail shells beneath my feet. Blue lights bounce
on the dark street: to Gary and Phil in their green uniforms,
forging animals from puffed-up latex gloves,

to the hospital parking bay, to pushing our way into theatre
through swing doors. I kiss the bruises, mauve on white
from the IVs, and think of the snails that were hurt as I ran.

They will find me in the street in my dressing gown

The next time I leave some of myself behind
in his cot or her hospital bed,
they will find me in the street in my dressing gown.

Paving slabs splintered at my feet. Spoiled water
the colour of rust. The name I used to call myself
written in chalk and washed away.

My heart burned to ash by the dreamers in the forest,
naked beneath their terry-cloth crowns.

The magician's daughter

She sits in tepid water six inches deep,
throws her hands out like she's catching birds.

"One... two... three, ladies and gentlemen... abracadabra!"
Her eyes are mint ice cream, pooled and sticky,

blonde curls tattered flags. A mess of freckles.
Her salt-and-vinegar frown.

On beauty

"Am I beautiful?" she asks, and my heart
stiffens in spasmodic rhythm, an extra –

to notice how clear her eyes are, khaki irises
in a black-lash frame, or sugared almonds

laid softly on satin. Stroke the kitten fur
of her cheek, count nineteen freckles
darting across her nose like rabbits in a field
of my imagining, that beauty spot, a warren at her jaw.

My fingers stroll luxuriously across her forehead,
brows knitted, helter-skelter like the slide
on the ArcelorMittal Orbit, 178m of meshed red steel.

– "Am I, Mummy? Am I beautiful?" –

(The soft pink of her lips is a sunset so unique
there's a kind of horror in it.)

I wear my keys like a glove

as we walk, hand in hand, feet crackling over leaves.
Their metal kiss is my armour, heavy brass my bayonet.
Their jagged edges are knives I'll use to protect you
in this forest of gold and green and a Faraway tree

that spills spell-words like Silky and Moon-Face
and the riotous, crashing Saucepan Man
and Jo and Bessie and Fanny – *wisha-wisha-wisha.*
Here, we are both six.

"Look!" You point to the dark trees
where you see an ordinary man, standing ordinarily.
I see a golem, a monster in the woods,
and my heart is a hare.

I draw you closer, force your small legs faster,
faster, faster until we fly, cover your ears to stop
his siren song of loneliness and need and wanting –
my keys, blades in my hand.

Higher, Mummy, higher

"When I'm not with you," she says, "I don't feel love."
I want to tell her she made me whole,

that when she was born, so was I.
Inside, a burning.

How do I tell her that when we're at the playground,
words shimmy to the top of the climbing frame,

stanzas tumble from the slide, skin their knees
and it is like a haunting?

The mothers scream into the void

as the children scream on the trampoline.
Their ghost faces line the windows, clutch
tea with violin fingers, their smoke-ring mouths.

Listen: the high-pitch, cat cries rise up
with helium softness, and down, weighted by peril.
Only the young are so alive with temporality.

God-like, a giddy keening for one giant bounce
to send them to the moon, gunshot into forever-orbit.
The mess of childhood is long, and bloody.

The mothers know this. They stand behind glass,
sorrow burning their throats, wishing (not wishing)
for a fall. For something to ripple the surface

of TV and "he'll only eat turkey dinosaurs", "I had it first" and "she
doesn't like beans touching the plate"...
In the forest, a howling.

The mothers prick up their ears, tongues
slide over teeth, bare and glistening.
They watch while one of the children commands the others

to line the inside of the trampoline like gladiators,
to throw their bodies in the air with brittle urgency,
to the death, always to the death. The mothers sense rupture.

Shuffle to the glass, breath damp and ragged, jostling for space,
elbows sharp as knives. Hold their breath and wait – "oh, god,
please" – for the children to land.

The pigeon in the church window

has forgotten how to sing. Got stuck in stained glass
for three heroic days until I couldn't bear it –
I changed the way I walked to go around the park instead.

Sometimes I get off the Tube at Leytonstone
so I don't have to see the sad smile of the *Big Issue* seller,
hear about her latest cancer or the baby's terrible asthma,
how he turns blue at night, drowned by his own lungs.
"I sometimes think it would be better if I died."

I can still see bits of it poking through the metal grill,
a shadow that killed itself with sunlight. Three days.
Three days was all it took.
Now they've turned the old church into flats.

This is what happens to a mother

when she's no longer in gainful employment,
when mothering is a synonym for heartbreak

and "what do you want for dinner?" a war cry,
empty as the fridge. She spreads herself thin

like butter, wears a coat of moss, pours summer fruits
into a glass beaker that tumbles through fingers

leaving a Rorschach of bloodstains on the tiled floor.
Watch: she wobbles as she decants herself

into the ice-box, a pink-jelly placenta.
Your love came out kicking –

and all night she bears your weight.
Her arms a vice as you lie damp, milk-heavy,

her tongue a frayed rope.
The burden of your kisses gnaws at her

like the scissor teeth of a hundred baby rats
in an ecstasy of biting.

This house, this gingerbread house.
One knock and it all falls down – or else, is eaten.

L'appel du vide

When I became *mother* I lost myself (*active*), I got lost (*passive*)
my mind broke and I went mad; I was mental, you know?

I couldn't cope with the horror of loving this tiny thing
so completely, it was like being INSIDE the news – like a hostage

situation, where I'm the gunman and the bullet,
where my life is narrated by David Attenborough;

where David Attenborough is talking, talking, talking, as I am
swallowed whole like a snake swallows a deer – inch by inch –

until the deer is no longer a deer, but a giant bulge
in the snake's stomach, and *Jesus Christ*, is it alive in there?

Could it still be alive in there?
Becoming a mother after seven series of *Gilmore Girls*,

while *baby* slept 23 hours of every day,
while *daughter* went to school and came home crying

because she had to make all new friends and couldn't hug me
because my hands were full of new baby, my breasts

full of milk, and it hurt for her to grip me tight
with her pink-and-green bracelet arms.

After they both got sick, heartbeats angry white-on-black:
      170 – "no, you can't go home" –
      200 – "we need to move you into resus" –

after that, a long time after that, while walking in the forest,
I realised I hadn't thought about the autumn leaves.

Hadn't noticed the gold and red and soft brown crunch,
or the swans or that heron sitting on the post

in his grey overcoat, or the dogs running sideways
with the wind in their ears, or the bluebells in the woods

that people travel for miles to see. I hadn't spoken for days,
I'd hardly eaten, and my mouth was a stone. Then I lost

myself somewhere between the bus stop and the A406,
on that motorway bridge where traffic zooms by so fast it blurs –

what's the word for the feeling when you stand too close
to the edge and get an uncontrollable urge to throw yourself off?

Café Diana

In Hyde Park, next to a cold, marble Victoria,
children in high-vis vests kick a ball around.

I leave picture galleries and breaking news of civil war
and goats that sing opera and "that'll do well on social"

to walk home through Notting Hill, past the Café Diana
with its red façade. Diana in hats, Diana in a crown,

sultry Diana in low-cut eighties black. Wistful
Diana on the steps of Kensington Palace,

sad at Northwick Park, bouquets
and blue gingham on a Bahrain airstrip.

Lonely Diana, with nobody to talk to on the phone.

Slow news day

In the stuffy newsroom, the scent of salt lingers between lines.
The Aegean laps hungrily at spaces while deflating rubber

dinghies sail on inky seas, crash into margins. Children stumble
shoeless over sentences and double-page spreads,

as fifty bodies float away from boats commanded by painters
who have never drawn sails before. Map-less, compass-less,

they pray their way towards Samos, only to overturn
20 yards from shore, a shallow, breakout box of statistics.

Ten souls – four babies, a cartoon boy on a black-and-white beach
in Turkey and the outline of a little girl, washed up

a few miles from Kusadasi.
For a while we care, clutch our own more tightly,

thank "God" or "luck" for England.
Then we call back our rescue ships, put away our whistles,

forget the flotilla, talk of "tackling immigration".
And when the next boat sinks, we'll put down our pens,

leave life vests at the bottom of the page,
an S. O. S (in brackets). Someone, please, bring us a shooting

at a school in midtown white America. Angry, loner, virgin
killer – now that, we can really get excited about.

This sad story will make you cry

A bridesmaid has a heart attack at her sister's £70,000
wedding on the exact same fucking day a poet visits

a nursing home. A sea, the poet says. A sea of outstretched hands.
If that doesn't make you cry, nothing will.

In Australia, a woman with dementia disappears,
one neat pile of bones left next to the water,

and I wonder if she was trying to make a friend in that black
lagoon, or if she fell in love while gazing at her own reflection.

A team of scientists sends a Tunnock's Tea Cake into space.
"We're delighted," they say, "over the moon!" *I cry, I cry, I cry.*

*

I *don't* cry when the paramedics lie about the sirens,
and they know I know. "Nothing to worry about," they say.

"Gets us there a bit faster, that's all." I watch them:
holding breaths, turning on the flashing lights, swapping

glances like lovers swap saliva as they shift into fourth gear.
I don't cry, sitting next to a hospital gurney while my love lies

helpless, chest moving up and down like an accordion played
fast and wild. I don't cry, pacing alone in an off-white cubicle

for seven hours, listening to the quiet unravelling
of a fourteen-year-old girl with wrists like ribbons.

I once asked an eye doctor if red-hot lasers
could make me see more clearly. Want to know what he said?

"Your tear ducts are so low," shaking his head.
"You'll never have 20/20 vision."

Ladybirds

Some mothers tell their daughters they love them
but don't love being mothers, and it makes me wonder

whether saying, "you've put on weight that doesn't suit you;
you've turned into a right little bitch, do you know that?"

is what love is – and if it is, then how do those daughters stop
themselves from shrinking down so small

that they fall between the gaps in old floorboards like lint
or dirty pennies or the tiny, desiccated bodies of ladybirds?

Some mothers stop speaking to their daughters for a month
for something they don't remember. They waltz nauseously

around the kitchen, unpack themselves into the dishwasher,
do cartwheels in the space reserved for knives –

those mothers see their soap-sud blood and say, "that's alright",
with corners, and it isn't alright at all.

Some daughters come home from university
and tell their mothers about an abortion

– not theirs, not their not-baby – and the mothers say,
"what a stupid thing to do." And they know, these daughters,

that they could never tell of their own not-babies,
if they did/didn't have them.

Patsy Palmer is not my mum, but I wish she was

Patsy Palmer is not my mum, even though a photo exists
of the two of us inexplicably posing next to a Thorntons
gingerbread heart with piped icing that says *Happy Mother's Day*.
Every year, on Mother's Day, I repost it without explanation,
and it's my lifelong dream that one day

people will think that Patsy Palmer *is* my mum,
even though it's impossible, unless Patsy had me
when she was eight. And I don't wish that kind of tragic
Guinness World Record on anyone, let alone Patsy,
but I *do* wish we were related.

I used to think it was a sign that as Bianca in *EastEnders*
she'd always call for Ricky, when my surname is Richards.
Sometimes at school utter cunts would call me "Vicky Ricky",
with the "Ricky" bit drawn out just like Patsy used to,
and I pretended to laugh, though my fingers were guitar strings

twanging nervously in E flat, and my throat
swallowed itself and I spent a disproportionate amount of time
wondering if that would count as suicide.
And when it's late at night and I can't sleep for thinking of things
like that: about snakes and all the people I've loved

but don't love any longer and what would happen if your car
was controlled remotely by a key and you were driving along
the motorway and chucked that key out of the window –
what would happen – on *those* nights,
when sleeping pills don't touch the sides

because my mind is so busy imagining what it would be like
to have sex with CBeebies presenters, and whether Mr Tumble
talks about going to *Justin's House* and uses it as a euphemism,
I would go to the one person who would hold me and stroke
my hair and tell me everything was going to be okay:

Patsy Palmer. That would be Patsy's job.

If Patsy were my mum, she'd smile a special smile every time
someone said it was funny I hadn't inherited her red hair
or freckles, and she'd pinch my cheeks and give me
a special look that meant: I love you anyway.

If someone's real mum said she loved them because she had to
but didn't like them very much, I'd offer up Patsy as an example
of what mothers should be, because Patsy would *never*
do that. My spiritual mum, my emotional support animal mum:
Patsy Palmer. Is 40 too old to be adopted?

I remember her in espadrilles

She came off the swing in dignified near-silence, cheek against gravel. A simple "oh!" like a bunch of flowers turning up at the door, unexpected. Crumpled, prostrate. I saw her thus: as a pilgrim at the Potala Palace, a snow angel. Arms splayed, the thick cable-twists of her hair. Her body a symphony, blood trickling from her cheek, a black swan. One shoe of canvas and esparto rope. The other – impossibly – metres away, her foot turned savage. The purple bruise of her lips, kissed and swollen. The blueness of her eyes, reflecting the clouds.

How you got that scar

I am David Blaine suspended over the Thames in a Perspex box for 44 days, I am my grandmother's compact mirror with its sickly powder breath, I am that Dartington crystal wine glass, a wedding gift, smashed to pieces. You are fighting to get away, to "What's that bang? What is a bang? What makes a bang happen?" You laugh even as you pull on your right ear, which I know means you're tired, or shy, or afraid, look at me sideways to check the ceiling of the world hasn't caved in, that this house, the heart of this house hasn't fractured, and I grin to hide the fact that I'm more fragile than I've ever been. The cat walks by. Your eyes crinkle at the edges like the lines on male faces three generations before you. "Gentle," I murmur. "Gentle." But you haven't learned to be gentle, yet. Come away clutching clumps of black fur, eyes incandescent with disbelief, fingers splayed. The cat has gone. In six months he'll fight back, glorious retribution carved two inches long into the peach-fuzz of your cheek. Twenty-three years from now a lover will spot it in the light of a bedside lamp that's turned towards the ceiling as you lie on a bedspread of forget-me-nots. He or she will trace the faint line with a nail that is slightly too sharp and ask, "What happened?" and you'll shrug and say you can't remember.

You won't remember any of this

I blow in the baby's face and he stops crying, bolts
backwards, throws his hands up in the air.

I do it again, he does it again.
I've never seen a face so perfect, so entirely mine.

This, this. This is the love I've read about.

Part III: Thunderstorms

I matched with Jesus on Hinge

He wears a crown of thorns in his profile picture,
says he's the Messiah (and maybe he is) but
maybe he's one of those guys who tells you
he can't decide between you and three other women,
because it's "hard", and can't everybody have a piece of Him?

Isn't that fair? Can't we all just "share" His love,
like He once shared two fish with the starving five thousand,
performed a "miracle ffs", drank a faceful of holy cum
(cum all ye faithful) quenched your thirst and also starved you,
watched you walk on the brittle surface of the lake, watched

you take your clothes off for drowning because drowning
is "so fucking hot" and what can you possibly do
with a boyfriend with stigmata – when the nails
run from his flesh straight into yours and in the pulsing
of your shared blood the only pain that's taken away is His?

At Milk Thistle

"Nikka from the Barrel is gorgeous," the barman says, but he puts
his hand on my knee and I taste smoke and confusion.

His fingers are hieroglyphs, each one a mollusc
suffocated by the rock it chose – the rock it loved

for a thousand years, covered in barnacles. They are like
those angler fish I read about, the ones with jagged teeth.

If I tilt my head in a certain way, the feet of a couple
on a first date don't quite meet at the bar.

He wears a black-check bow-tie; she's in a red-and-white ghost
dress burned into her skin by the sun.

They steal glances as they steal sips of champagne
while the women next to them talk without speaking,

conversation like mirrors.
The barman brings them a drink but doesn't touch their knees

and I want – "What? What do you want?" –
to sit in the quiet dark, in a ghost dress of my own.

Ingrid Bergman

Ingrid Bergman is so beautiful that when I watch her
in *Casablanca* I want to peel her skin off and wear it as a coat.

Pluck out her eyes, like Goneril ordered Cornwall to do
to Gloucester – "leave him to my displeasure."

I dream heavy, sexy dreams of rolling one of Ingrid's eyes
against my tongue like that gobstopper I kept for weeks

in a plastic pot of precious things: stones pulled from a stream
in South Africa, a sparkly button, two baby teeth, a crumpled

crisp packet dropped by the boy I loved. Ingrid Bergman's
glorious, gobstopper-eye makes my tongue ache

the way it aches when you eat pineapple, because of bromelain.
It lures you in with its sticky sweetness

and eats you alive. But Ingrid Bergman's eye doesn't
last long; I can't help those furtive licks.

It grows small and wrinkled, stops shining, and then the tears
dry up. Lost on a bed of sequins prised from a polyester coat.

My precious precious things: a ring, a postcard,
nail scissors, an old shell. A letter from my father.

Stendhal Syndrome

When I think about you
I am seized with fierce palpitations of the heart.
An attack of nerves – like Stendhal was,
overcome by the nearness of those great men:

Machiavelli, Michelangelo, Galilei.
Close enough to feel their granite kiss,
rough against his fingers. Torn apart
by a few hundred years (a trivia of longing).

When I think about you
I ache for the tourists in Florence,
dizzy with desire for David,
for his marble heart. His sightless eyes

turned towards Rome, warning lovers
and would-be-lovers to be careful.

Roxanne

We fell in love at one in the morning
– the easiest time of day to fall in love –

in a snooker hall in Beckton.
She potted the yellow, then the red, even though

she wasn't supposed to. "Live local?" she asked
and I wanted to tell her I'd run away with her

there and then, but I knew that once the game stopped,
she'd tell me I was being distant, hiding something.

That she didn't trust the shapes I saw in the clouds:
a bear, a fox. My grandmother's broken watch.

CBeebies has a lot to answer for

She asks questions you wouldn't think of asking:
"How do you make a bouncy castle?" "How cold
is the ice on an ice rink?" "How does a toilet flush?"

Sometimes she scrunches up her eyes like she's seen a magpie
making love in a nest of razor blades, sometimes
her yellow hair reminds me of a noose –

Maddie Moate won a BAFTA for her work hunting
prehistoric shark teeth, for teaching kids about bones
and the world's largest, smelliest flower.

She even went to Bali for a month to find out how rice grows.
Oh, Maddie, Maddie Moate – for you I'd write poetry
with wax crayons from the factory you showed us

in series one, scrawl sonnets across the walls of an old church.
I'd hide love-letters in cans of beans and throw them
out to sea for sharks with tin-opener teeth to swallow

whole until they rattle deep inside a child's nightmares,
because they watched *Jaws* when they weren't supposed to,
because it was the seventies and red-froth blood

didn't hurt as much thirty years ago. Maddie Moate
– the woman I love/am in love with – has had a terrible time
with her skin (I watched her vlog about it).

Sometimes it flares up so badly she has to spend five hours
in make-up to be able to say, "I love the way
he paints a monkey on the plastic, don't you?"

while bouncing up and down on fifty sheets
of rainbow-coloured polyvinyl. I once tweeted her to ask
where she got her amazing red trainers but she didn't reply

and I felt like getting myself lost in the nearest desert

just so they'd do a TV report about me, just so she'd notice,
but I've never been very good at practical things like survival

or saying what I want (or don't want) or putting together
Ikea furniture. I once made a chair and screwed
all three legs on upside-down; I once thought

about using the train tracks as a pillow – I am in love
with a woman who doesn't know I exist,
and sometimes I don't know if I do.

Will you please? *

I know we've just met, but you smell delicious
and I want to grab your hair
and force you down between my knees, breathe you in

until the clouds rattle dangerously,
until flamenco dancers snap their staccato heels –
I know we've just met, but will you please ask me to marry you?

I won't say yes. But I'll want to,
and when I'm old and soft as a photograph
that's been folded too many times and stuffed inside a wallet

next to a love note from a long-dead child that spells
happiness exactly the wrong way, I'll think of you
and get the same feeling I get now, thinking of you.

The same delicious anticipation of what might be,
what could have been if you weren't you, and I wasn't here,
the forest looming – wild, so wild! – at my back.

* *The first line of this poem borrows from the opening of Kim Addonizio's 'Party'.*

Dean Gaffney

The first person to ask me out on a dating app
was Dean Gaffney, and when people ask why I didn't
swipe right – didn't leap straight out of the salmon settee
my parents owned in the 1990s, the one I once brought
a boy home to who rocked and moaned on top of me

fully clothed until we both came while watching *Forrest Gump*...
the one another boy who had joined the army fingered me on
while giving me glandular fever that lasted
all of my first year of uni, where I had tonsillitis 12 times,
once a month, like a period, like a horoscope...

that sofa, the one I lay on with my face swollen like marshmallow,
my wisdom teeth ripped out and bleeding,
my giant fluffy cat slippers, Boston City Sports T-shirt in extra,
extra large... *that* sofa, the one my parents were sitting on
when I stood and walked away after consciously deciding

not to kiss them goodnight because I felt all of a sudden
too old to kiss them goodnight, but I didn't notice the way
their hearts broke as I lurched dizzily from the room,
adulthood measured in steps to the kitchen... *that* sofa:
the one I ordered double pepperoni pizza from on Fridays

with my best friend who's now an Orthodox Jew, so the fact
we ate pepperoni *on* Friday nights is not to be brought up
at the dinner table on Shabbat... *that* sofa, the one
my legs would stick to in the summer heat,
when my whole body was sticky-legged heat...

and Forrest Gump kept running and running
and dry humping and cumming – so when people ask me why
I didn't swipe right on Dean Gaffney, I tell them
it's because I couldn't face sex chat that involved
asking him if he's "Wellard" yet,

or touching him square *on* his Prince Albert,

or roleplay where he's Frank and I'm Pat Butcher...
but what I don't say is that I was frightened Dean might tell me
after two delicious dates that I'm "too much",
that he wants a girl who "doesn't take life too seriously",

that he wants "something casual", when poets can't *do* casual,
we aren't even casual about clouds...and how can we be "casual"
when even the shadow of a leaf in certain light
can tear us limb from heartbroken limb, reduce us
to a puddle of liquid mercury on the floor

like those weird creatures from *The Abyss*: heads protuberant
like a penis, bodies useless static on the street,
bowled over by the terrible beauty of life and love
and mortality in all its forms? I said all of this to Dean Gaffney.
Dean Gaffney didn't reply.

In love with the Greens

I see her first at the supermarket, weighing eggs in aisle three,
bobbing the delicate ovals against her palm.
She puts down the one with feathers, another

with a spiderweb of cracks. Smiles as she selects a box
that's smooth, intact. How I wish I could be the egg held
between thumb and forefinger against the starched white

of her collar. Pressed against her dress, her lemony scent.
Then *he* strides by, devastating in navy. Pauses to tug her
ponytail while she flushes and pretends not to watch

him walk away. Their smiles are knives against my goose flesh.
I drink her in – watch her watch him turn right
at aisle five, then I crumple next to laundry starch

and yellow, cheering Marigolds, lust stacked high like boxes
of cat food. I've never wanted to watch someone's back
in the supermarket as much as Mrs Green

wants to watch her husband's. The Greens, the lovely Greens:
I follow them home from the conveyor-belt checkout, cross
the cobblestones set in 1876, that old church, the village hall

where I've never seen a play. Turn my pain
into shadow puppets as I imagine them in bed together
because I'm a masochist and crave every lashing.

And the reason it hurts is because with every stroke
they're not wanting me, and don't want me
for at least five, ten, fifteen minutes

while they're slowly fucking, and they fuck and fuck
until: *la petite mort.*
(The Greens got married in Paris, I think.)

For when Mr Green shudders and comes inside Mrs Green,

and she sighs and says his name three times, clutching
his head to her breasts like rosary beads –

it is *their* petite mort, but it's also mine.
It is mine.
The night is a quiet symphony.

*

I walk down the lane, tip-toeing over gravel, and wonder
 what I'll say if the Greens ask me to join them. It could
be so warm, pressed against her leg, his hand on mine,

kissing them both goodnight. Turning our heads
like swallows, fingers tangled in a heap across my thigh.
The thought drives me wild but also makes me want to die

because I know that in the morning, when I get up to leave,
while Mrs Green makes coffee and Mr Green hums
– and he can't sing, and it doesn't matter –

they'll catch each other's eye and smile, the way they did
on their wedding day in probable Paris or a small but
unfathomably romantic crumbling church in Wales.

And the morning after I spend the night with the Greens,
the winter sunlight will burn her hair and Mr Green
will be consumed with love, with tender longing

for the life he has with her, with Mrs Green, and *she* will give
thanks for September and bluebells and apricots and warm bread
and pistachios and sweet, tender, achingly vanilla sex.

As I follow them home I think – no, I *know* –
that if I had a little of what they have, I could be happy.
We could be happy.

This is not a valentine

because valentines are paper roses and Lindt
and fluffy bears that say things like *I wuv you.*

They're set menus and pink champagne and Groupon
deals for nights away at a spa hotel in Swindon,

where the maid leaves chocolate on the sheets
next to an origami swan that's actually a flannel.

Sometimes it's a napkin. And it's looking
out of the window and seeing people playing golf,

the screams of kids in a walled garden. Valentines
are taking a walk with the dog on Sunday

and booking a family holiday to Tenerife
and talking about where to retire, and when,

and won't it be nice when the kids are grown
and we can spend more time together –

won't that be nice? And it would. It would be nice.
This is not a valentine. Valentines are anniversaries

and sex on birthdays and a favourite perfume,
bought in Duty Free. They're cards that say

"I'm yours", signed with a pet name used for years,
so long you can hardly remember how it started.

I'm yours. But this is not a valentine.

Wild

There is a tree in the forest I want more than any other.
And every morning when I see it standing there
– tall, broad, branches flexed like biceps –
I sigh, and it is a benediction.

I'd like to rub myself against its trunk, over and over,
and sometimes I do, when I'm out running,
but I pretend I'm stretching my hamstring.
Give a small wave to the other runners (the way 'runners' do).

Flex my thigh. Mouth "cramp" and gesture downwards
without making a sound. They nod and smile and disappear,
and I can get back to what I was doing. What *was* I doing...?
Oh, yes. Rubbing myself against my tree.

Ha. Listen to me: "my" tree. It better be my fucking tree.
But, anyway. This tree. You should see it.
It's got so much chlorophyll, its roots are *this* thick,
it positively oozes sap –

People say it'll never work, that plants and humans
can't be happy; that they won't, can't, mustn't live together
in perfect, beach-hut-postcard contentment.
They're wrong. Look at Christmas trees.

And all I know is when I say my daily prayer, caught
in a beam of sunlight, nothing has ever been so beautiful.
My breath catches in my throat and I ache,
I ache for the scratch of rough bark.

One day, I'm going to marry that tree,
and drag its twigs home to bed with me
and wake up every single morning,
wet soil in my mouth, covered in dirt.

This is how we love in a pandemic

I want you tapped to the green throb of a screen
late at night where we lie stultified.
These heavy heartbeats keep time
with our frozen-dinner fatigue, our potato lust.

I miss you, thinking of your tongue
on my daily walk, prayers at the altar
of a tree-lined church. Swans bear
feathered witness to my dirty thoughts.

You can't see my unwashed hair,
my extra-large t-shirt, the perfume I dab
at my wrists like I'm mopping up blood
after cutting myself with your scent.

When I breathe, I breathe you in.
And this is how I imagine you: naked,
golden in the dawn light, one arm
scooping me to you like water.

In the pub he planned to buy as a child

the man I'm not allowed to love sits back and looks at me
as I tell a story about a friend whose husband told her

she was too "mother" to make love to, and how that hurt,
but doesn't hurt anymore, and what I don't say

(though my mouth keeps talking, my hands wave around
like they're spinning sugar) is that I can barely speak at all –

barely notice the taxidermy fox watching over us
from a glass box as if it's wondering what it is we all do

when we serve ourselves up like hors d'oeuvres,
hoping the other will like the taste. The taste of "us"

is a full or medium-bodied red some chef made up
in a busy kitchen, adding sweetness, desire, a splash

of melancholy. He went easy on commitment, notes the fox.
And it's hard to concentrate when he looks at me like that:

as though my face is a puzzle, my heart a game of sudoku
with an 8 at the centre. Hard to think about anything

but the way his eyes narrow at the edges, dark and delicate
as Marcona almonds imported from Spain, the exact

right angle of his cheek. The soft swell of his lips
with that bow in the middle, perfect for biting.

The thunder of his hand on mine.

Unspeakable acts of violence

It just happened

It didn't mean anything

She didn't mean anything

You don't mean anything

I never loved you

It was just sex

do anything nice?

we clash mugs around / fingers on the button for boiling water / "do anything nice?" / our smiles are knives / we turn them inwards / "oh, you know" / spent the afternoon in love / twisted, writhed / sheets damp with secrets / took love into my mouth / tasted wet-slick hope / "what about you?" / burnt my house down / lined up rows and rows of tiny bombs / filled them with hurt and pride and disappointment / let them explode / fire raged for hours / "me, oh" / ate dinner with my friend / told her about the war / hoped she'd help me duck for cover / find a hard hat or flak jacket / maybe an old air raid shelter / "not really" / forgot about collateral damage / she said I'm very selfish / said maybe I'm depressed / sympathy in rations / "nothing special" / picked shrapnel from my skin / sobbed into a pork-belly curry / the waiter said sorry over and over / said it back like we were singing a duet / wanted to tell him it wasn't my mouth that was burning / "nothing much" / but my whole life had gone up in flames / wanted to let him / douse me in cucumber yoghurt / wrap me in a shroud of sticky lime / bury me in chutney / "it was fine, you know" / we take our tea back to our desks / "the same as usual"

I burned his letters

But not the ones he wrote to me, for he never wrote me
a single word except once, early on, when in red pen

he scrawled *Victoria, you suck* and it was a joke,
but I stared for days at his handwriting

– the long slope of his *y*, the sexy, savage underscoring of his *k* –
and I knew then, way back, that he would rip

me open like ballpoint on recycled paper, scrawl his name
across my body in invisible ink, leave me hanging

like a contortionist in a cloud of long-eared, long-hatted rabbits,
then erase me like chalk on a blackboard,

leave me smeared, a white stain – the beautiful things
I wanted him to write forgotten like a rose.

they say the ocean is on fire

but
how can
water burn
how can the
gulf of mexico be
on fire I don't get it
don't get it at all how
can something so vast so
wet so deep go up in flames
how can it char turn to ash how
can salt get into a cut when you're
wearing a bandage wrapped around
your fourth finger a bandage wrapped
around your heart how can it get infected
the poison welling up like oil welling up like
tears how does it stop working when it worked
so well for so long or I guess I thought it did how can
it leave a scar a ridged welt of spiny humpbacked whales
another scar that won't fade how can a calf cling to a mother
when the mother is harpooned how do the waves sink a dingy
how can our waves sink a dingy carrying twelve frightened
children how can we turn
them away at
our borders how does a wound heal at its borders
how does skin ravaged by words heal how clean
is your knife how swiftly can you run it from
your wrist to mine how can I stop you
leaving how did it already happen
how are there wildfires in
the arctic I don't get
it at all please think
of the children

Handover notes

A morning bath is his favourite part of the day, a blast of opera, his tuneless voice, but he doesn't care, except when his brother points it out, when his cheeks flush though he doesn't say anything, just rubs his hands together like cymbals; still, sing he does, and did, to our daughter when she was born, stayed up until 3am on the hospital ward with her feet in his hands, crooning arias from *Carmen*; placed her in the Moses basket on that first night home, all wrapped up like a small, salty parcel of fish and chips, and we didn't know what we were doing, and we held each other as tightly as we held our breaths; bought her a tiny dress she wore once, then suddenly she was grown; taught her kindness, taught me kindness too, kindness even in the face of "I'm sorry" and "I can't do this anymore"; so be kind to him, please, be kind; especially in December, when he misses his mother so badly that he'll wear that old black hoody with the tattered sleeves and bitten zip for days, and won't come to bed, and he'll play *La Bohème*, her favourite, loud enough for it to thump through the floor like toothache; he'll eat rice and gravy when he's sad, I know it's weird but bear with him, swollen bowls of soft, white rice, because it's hard to chew when your heart is breaking, even harder to swallow; and if he needs you to hold him he won't say it but he'll hover in a doorway and say nothing, over and over, but nothing really means everything, nothing means love, so love him, please; love him and if there's anything else you want to know I'll tell you.

This is my last will & testament

When the time comes for me to die, put me in a lobster suit
like the guy at the end of the London Marathon,

for there is always that guy. Doughy flesh hidden by foam
and latex, smile wide and cheering. He pays extra

for comfort ventilation panels, a built-in cooling fan, googly eyes
(on springs). Claw mittens. A separate headpiece.

If I could spend one day inside that suit,
I would die happy.

Listen: pour boiling water over me, press the lid of the pan
down tight, steam-clean my secrets.

Put your fingers in your ears to drown out
my high-pitched whistling. Watch my white-blue flesh turn pink.

VICTORIA RICHARDS is Voices Editor at *The Independent*. She has been shortlisted in the Bath Novel Award and Lucy Cavendish College Fiction Prize, was highly commended for poetry in the Bridport Prize and came third in *The London Magazine* Short Story Competition 2017. In 2020, she came second in the Magma Poetry Competition and won the 'Nature in the Air' poetry competition. A selection of her work was published in *Primers: Volume Four* (Nine Arches Press, 2019). *You'll need an umbrella for this* is her debut collection. Follow her at www.twitter.com/nakedvix.